MAKE YOUR MARK

The Drawing Book for Children

Written and illustrated by Sarah Richardson

Tate Publishing

First published 2012 by order of the Tate Trustees
by Tate Publishing, a division of Tate Enterprises Ltd,
Millbank, London SW1P 4RG
www.tate.org.uk/publishing

Text, Illustration and photographs by Sarah Richardson 2012
All artwork copyright Sarah Richardson 2012

A catalogue record for this book is available from the British Library.

ISBN 978-1-84976-011-9

Designed by Wayne Campbell
Cover designed by Esterson Associates using artwork by Sarah Richardson
Reproduction by DL Imaging Ltd, London
Printed and bound in China by C&C Offset Printing Co., Ltd

Acknowledgements
JOHN AND MARGARET RICHARDSON

MAKE YOUR MARK

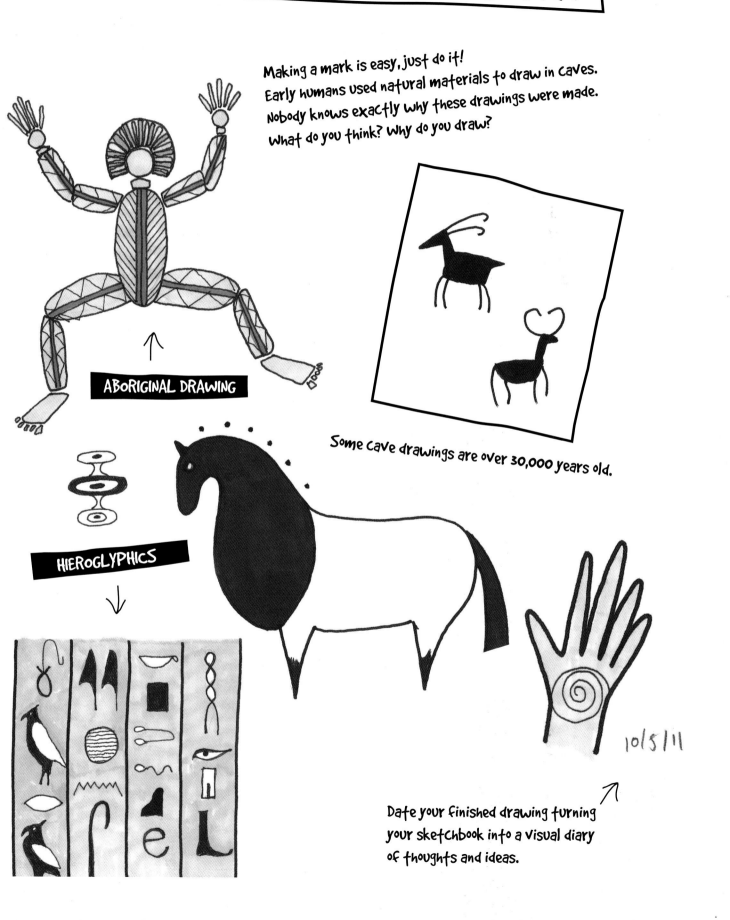

Making a mark is easy, just do it!
Early humans used natural materials to draw in caves.
Nobody knows exactly why these drawings were made.
What do you think? Why do you draw?

ABORIGINAL DRAWING

Some cave drawings are over 30,000 years old.

HIEROGLYPHICS

10/5/11

Date your finished drawing turning
your sketchbook into a visual diary
of thoughts and ideas.

WHAT TO DRAW ON

LONDON
28.01.11
E1

0 D
0 2
9 0
3 E
3 0
9 4
8 4

GREAT BRITAIN POSTAGE PAID
0025
PB825409

You don't have to draw in caves! Draw on different paper or in your sketchbook.

Stick your favourite drawings in your sketchbook so you don't lose them.

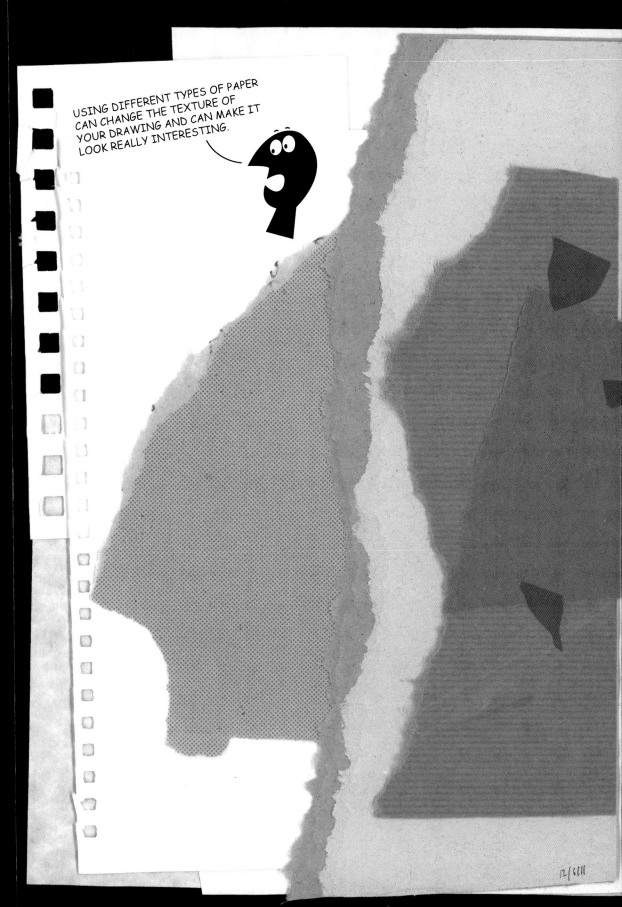

WHAT TO USE

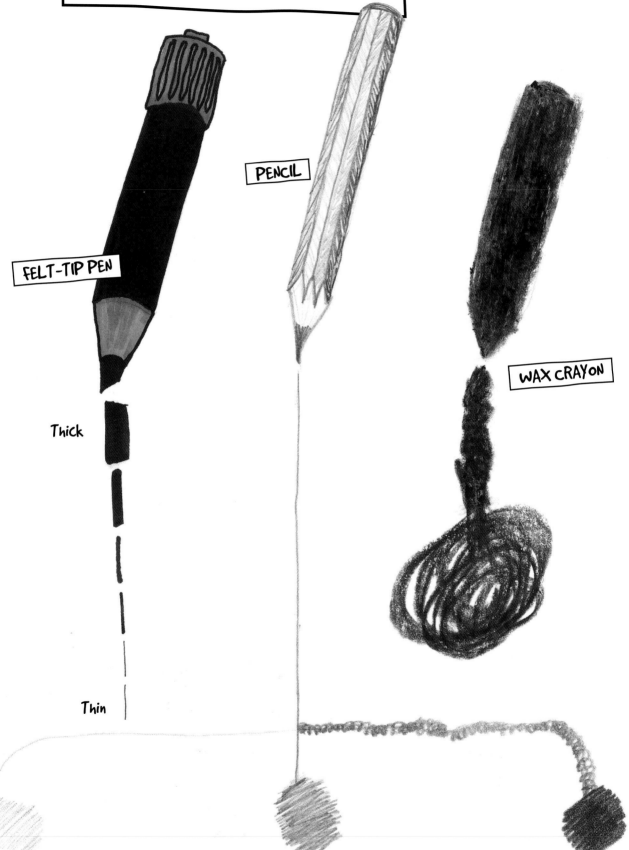

PENCIL

FELT-TIP PEN

WAX CRAYON

Thick

Thin

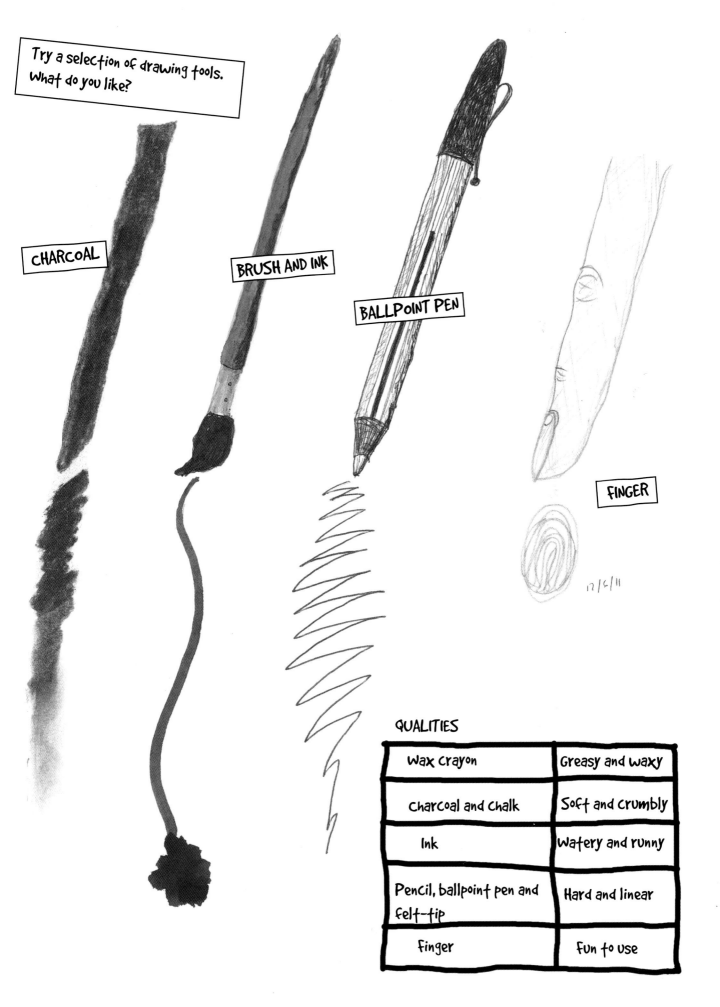

Try a selection of drawing tools. What do you like?

CHARCOAL

BRUSH AND INK

BALLPOINT PEN

FINGER

12/5/11

QUALITIES

Wax crayon	Greasy and waxy
Charcoal and chalk	Soft and crumbly
Ink	Watery and runny
Pencil, ballpoint pen and felt-tip	Hard and linear
Finger	Fun to use

TONE

THERE ARE DIFFERENT WAYS TO CREATE TONE.

CROSS HATCHING AND LAYERING

More layers = darker tone

HALF CLOSE YOUR EYES. THE AMOUNT OF LIGHT TRAVELLING INTO YOUR EYES IS REDUCED. THIS HELPS YOU TO SEE THE DIFFERENCE BETWEEN TONES MORE EASILY. TRY IT!

THICKNESS OF LINE

PRESSURE

Change the pressure.
Light pressure = light line
Pressing hard = dark line

SPACING

Lines   Dots   Dashes

close together = dark

further apart = light

Make inky fingerprints. Add details to change them into a new drawing.

Use the blunt end of a paintbrush to make dots.

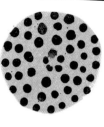

Drawing ink is very dark. Add water to make it lighter. This is called a wash.

Put some drops of ink on a piece of paper. Fold it in half. What can you see?

Drip a blob of ink onto the paper. Blow through a straw, and chase the ink into random lines. What does this remind you of?

RUBBINGS

EXPLORING MAKING RUBBINGS OF DIFFERENT SURFACES.

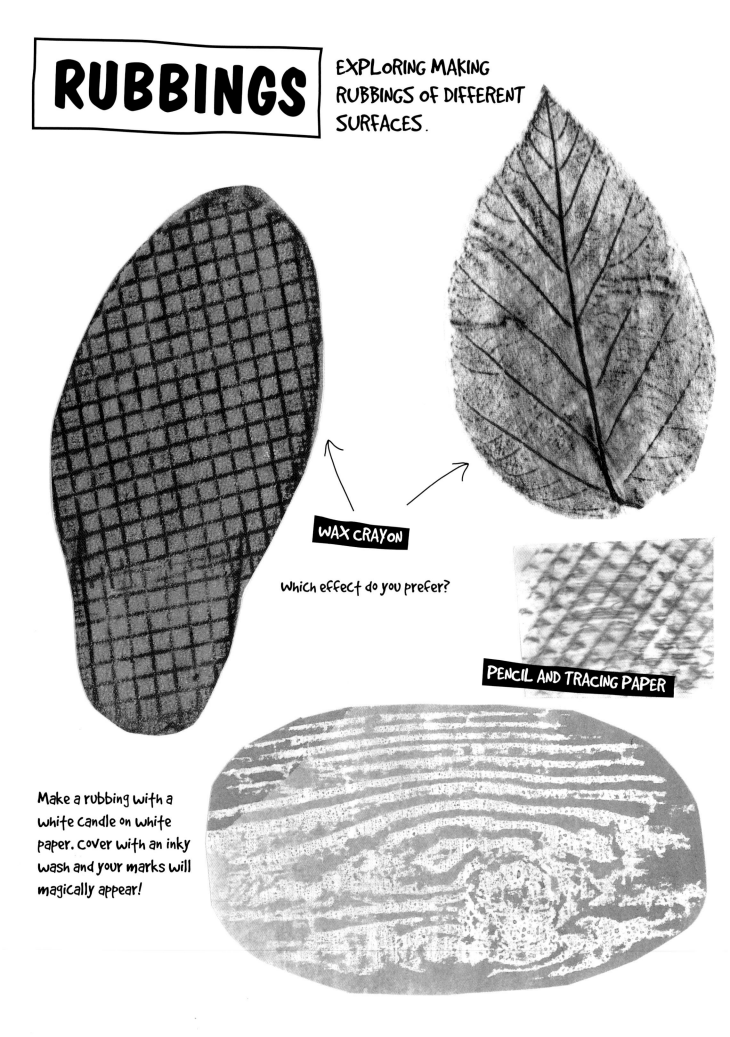

WAX CRAYON

Which effect do you prefer?

PENCIL AND TRACING PAPER

Make a rubbing with a white candle on white paper. Cover with an inky wash and your marks will magically appear!

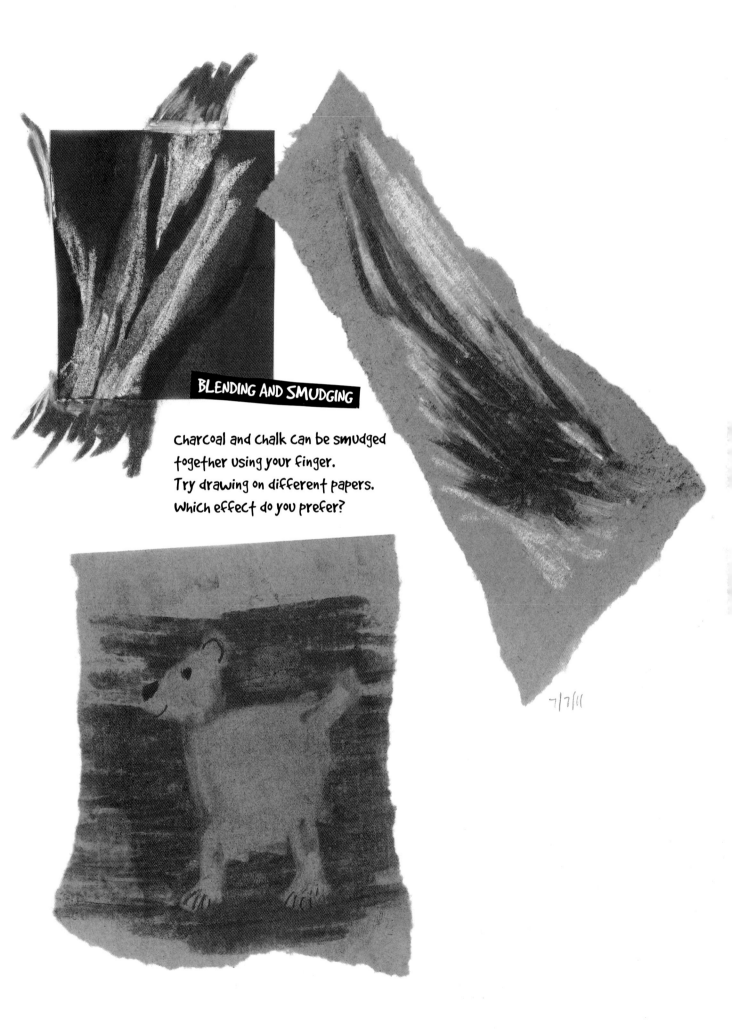

BLENDING AND SMUDGING

Charcoal and chalk can be smudged
together using your finger.
Try drawing on different papers.
Which effect do you prefer?

7/7/11

INSPIRATION

WHAT TO DRAW?

Everything and anything!! A blank page is ready for you to fill.

Look around you. Draw real things

or draw a feeling, a mood,

a memory, an experience, a wish or dream.

Record a story, a journey, a map, an idea, or a plan.

Play around with lines, shapes and doodles!

Let your imagination free!

You are the artist. You decide what to draw!

There are no limits...

A DRAWING HAS TO START SOMEWHERE. MAKE A MARK AND SEE WHERE IT TAKES YOU.

SCRIBBLING

Scribbling helps to get your creativity flowing and is a great way to warm-up the muscles in your hand, wrist and arm before drawing.

SCRIBBLING IS LIKE MESSY COLOURING-IN!

FILL A WHOLE PAGE WITH SCRIBBLE. BE FREE! GO ON! ENJOY!

2/7/11

Draw a scribble.
Add details and change it
into something new.

Draw a scribble. Try to copy it.

Scribbling has no rules.

Change your speed, direction and pressure as you move over the page.

Draw over your scribble.

Round and round

Up and down

Side to side

17/6/11

STRAIGHT LINES

FROM SCRIBBLE to A STRAIGHT LINE.

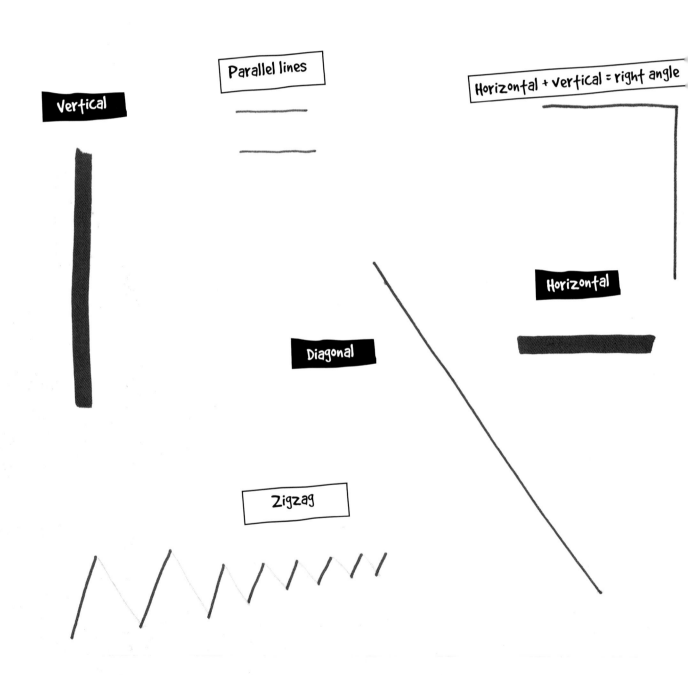

Parallel lines

Vertical

Horizontal + vertical = right angle

Diagonal

Horizontal

Zigzag

How to Draw a Straight Line (Without a Ruler)

1. Get ready for action; sit up straight!
2. Lock your wrist and fingers.
3. Stretch your arm forward.
4. Place your pencil on the paper.
5. Focus.
6. Bend your elbow towards your body, pulling your hand down the page.

PRACTICE WILL IMPROVE YOUR DRAWING.

Feel the movement in your shoulder as well as your elbow.

Straight lines make up our man-made world.

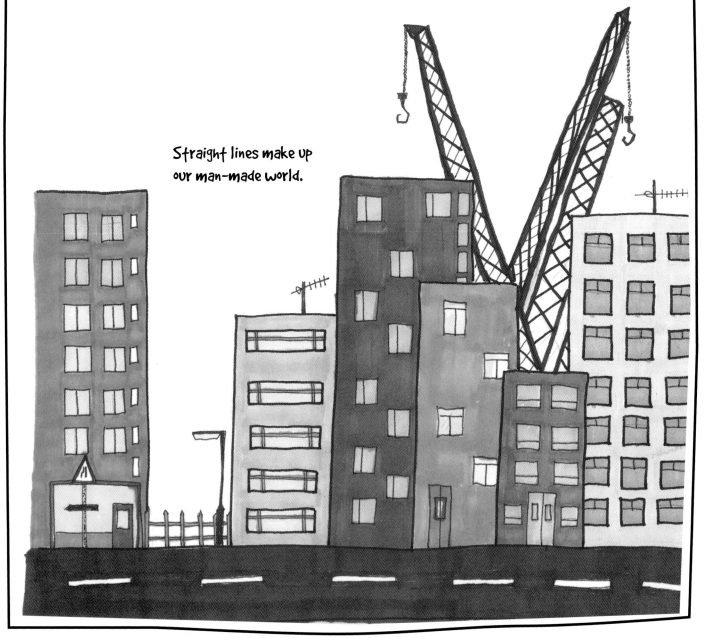

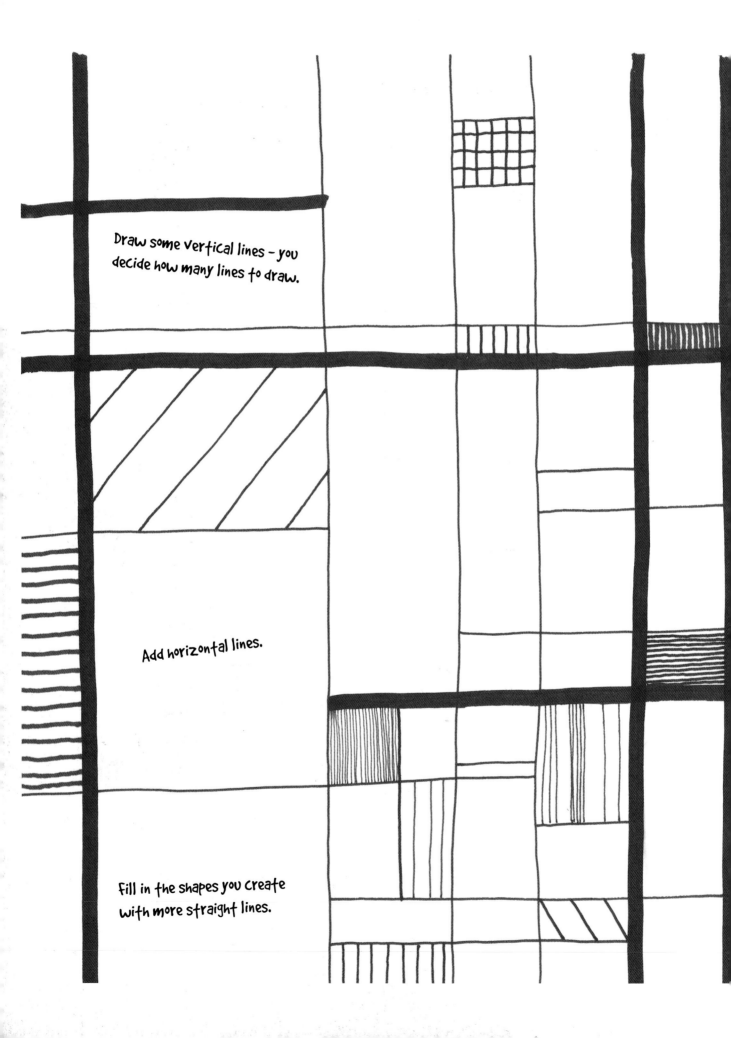

Draw some vertical lines – you decide how many lines to draw.

Add horizontal lines.

Fill in the shapes you create with more straight lines.

How many designs can you make only using two straight lines?

CHOOSE A DESIGN
TO MAKE A FLAG
FOR YOUR OWN
CASTLE.

Take a journey around the paper with your pencil.
Move up and down, left and right as you explore your page.
Aim to finish where you started.

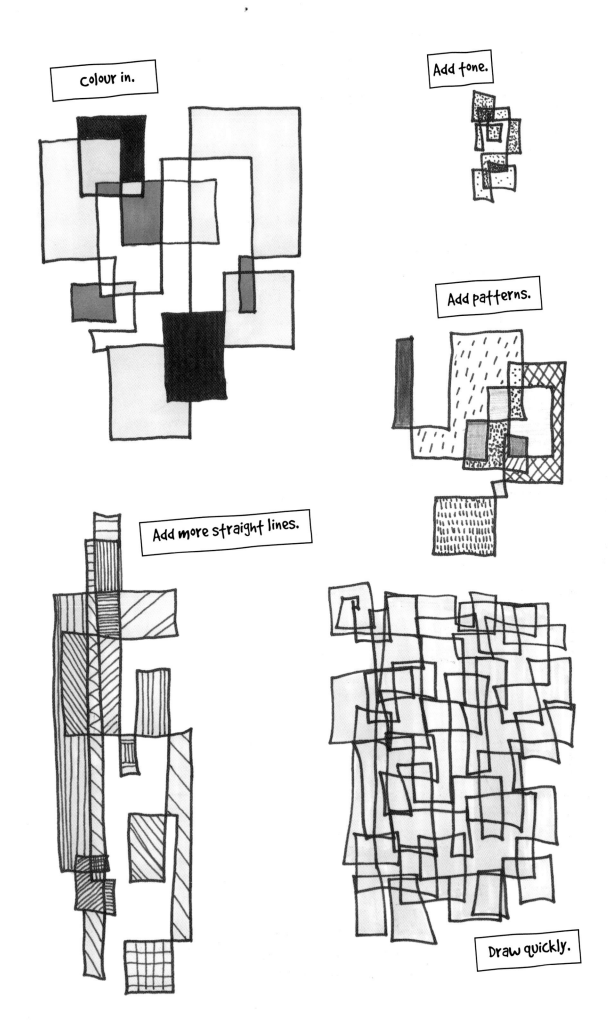

Colour in.

Add tone.

Add patterns.

Add more straight lines.

Draw quickly.

Arrows point and show direction.
Be an arrow detective. Look for
arrows when you are out and about.
Draw and record them!

CURVED LINES

A CURVED LINE IS THE OPPOSITE OF A STRAIGHT LINE.

UNLOCK your wrist and fingers...

keep your hand relaxed...

loose and flexible to make your curved line

curly

IF YOU CAN DRAW A STRAIGHT LINE AND A CURVE YOU CAN DRAW ANYTHING!

Bumpy

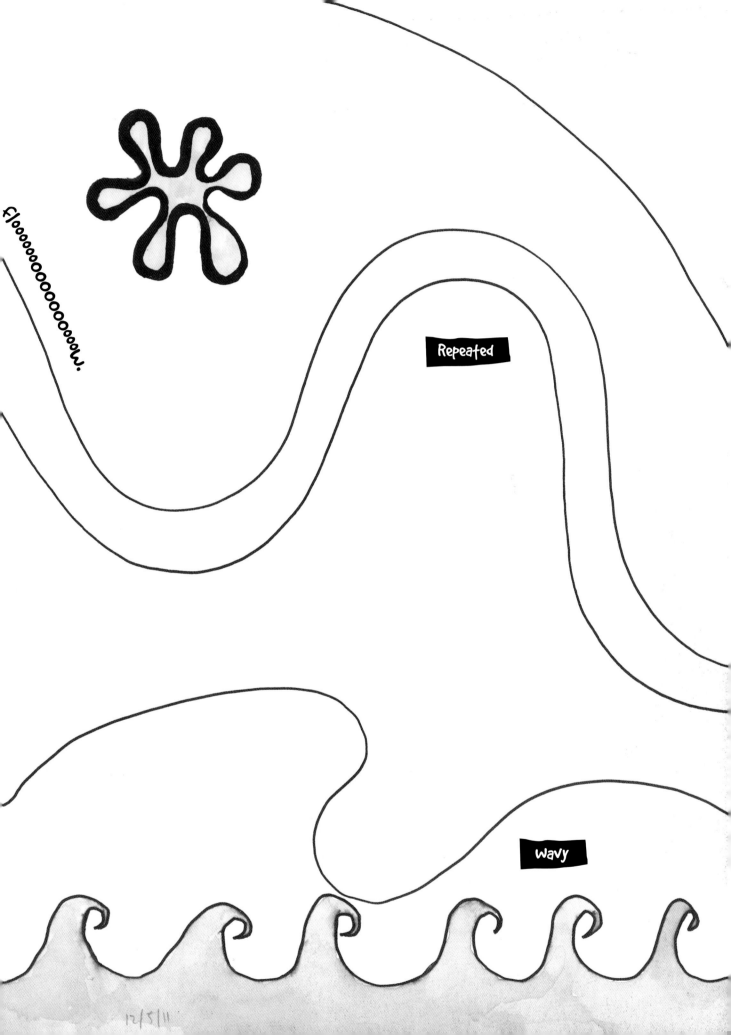

flooooooooooooow.

Repeated

wavy

12/5/11

CREATE YOUR OWN CURVED LINE PATTERNS. CHOOSE A NUMBER ... 6 and draw!

6 curved lines from one point.

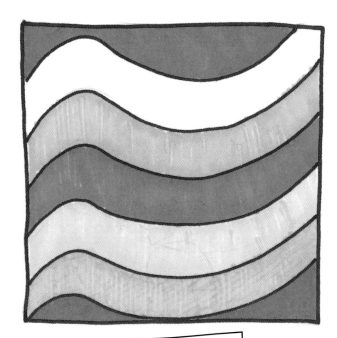

Colour in your patterns.

Repeated.

USE A DIFFERENT NUMBER AND YOUR PATTERNS WILL CHANGE.

Jump from side to side 6 times.

Add more patterns.

6 curves from the middle.

overlapping curves.

SPIRALS

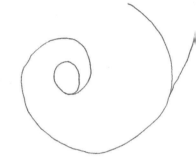

A SPIRAL IS A NEVER-ENDING CURVED LINE.

Why do spirals appear in drawings and designs in nearly every society in the ancient world?

Greeks

Egyptians

Mayans

Indians

Africans

Aboriginals

Celts

Maori

Research and draw!

See a spiral in action... watch how water disappears down the plug hole!

DRAWING SPIRALS

1. Draw light guidelines.

2. Start in the middle, draw round.

3. and round.

4. and round.

5. and round.

Fill your page with swirls, whirls and spirals.

NATURE GROWS IN SPIRALS...

that's why you do not see many straight
lines in the natural world.

CIRCLES

A CIRCLE IS A CURVED LINE THAT STARTS AND FINISHES IN THE SAME PLACE.

Not a proper circle because the line does not join.

An oval looks like a squashed circle.

Change a circle into a sphere by adding shadow.

A circle fits into a square.

Go round and round really fast to make circle patterns, big and small!
Can you draw using both hands at the same time? Have a go!

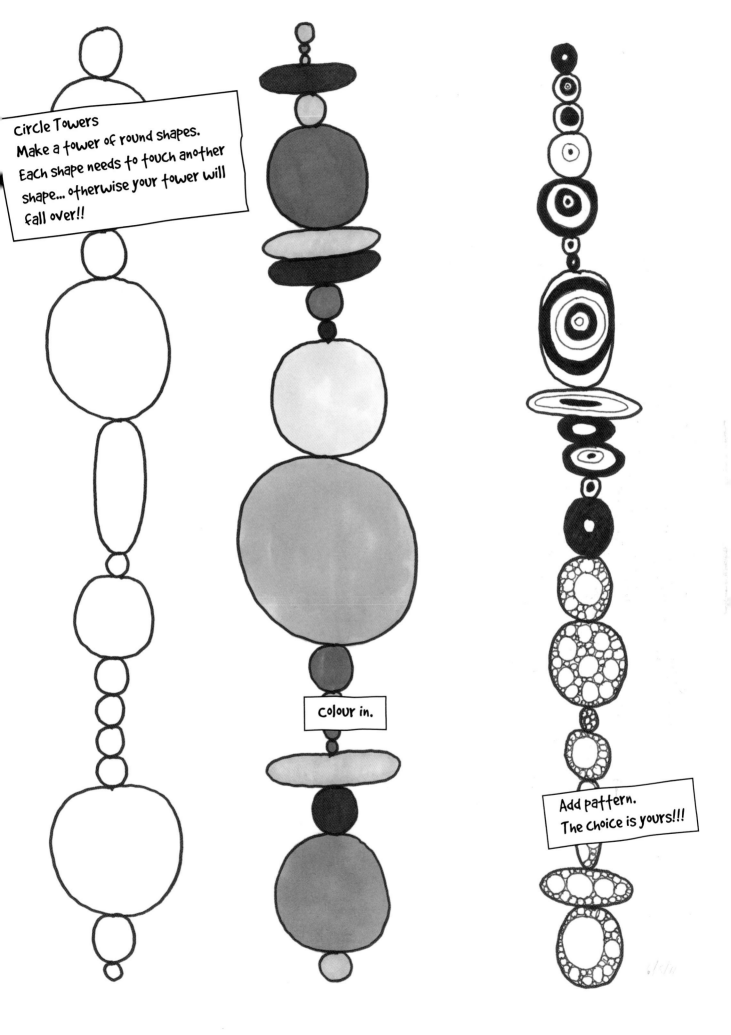

Circle Towers
Make a tower of round shapes.
Each shape needs to touch another
shape... otherwise your tower will
fall over!!

Colour in.

Add pattern.
The choice is yours!!!

DO YOUR SUMS

SHAPES ARE MADE FROM EITHER
STRAIGHT OR CURVED LINES AND
SOMETIMES BOTH.

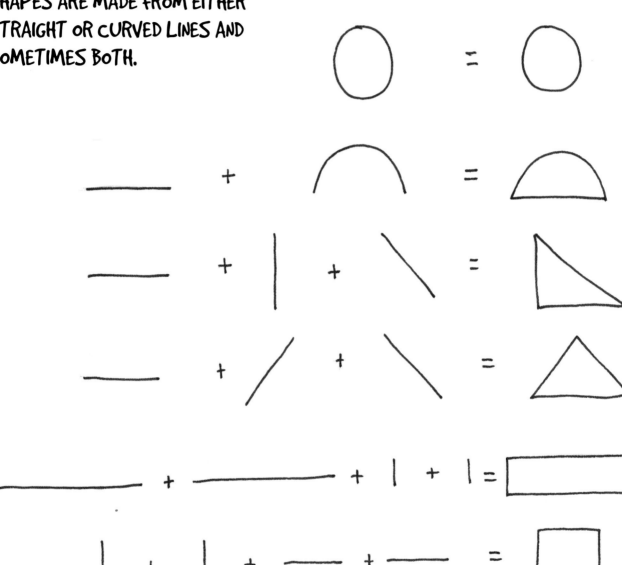

20/6/11

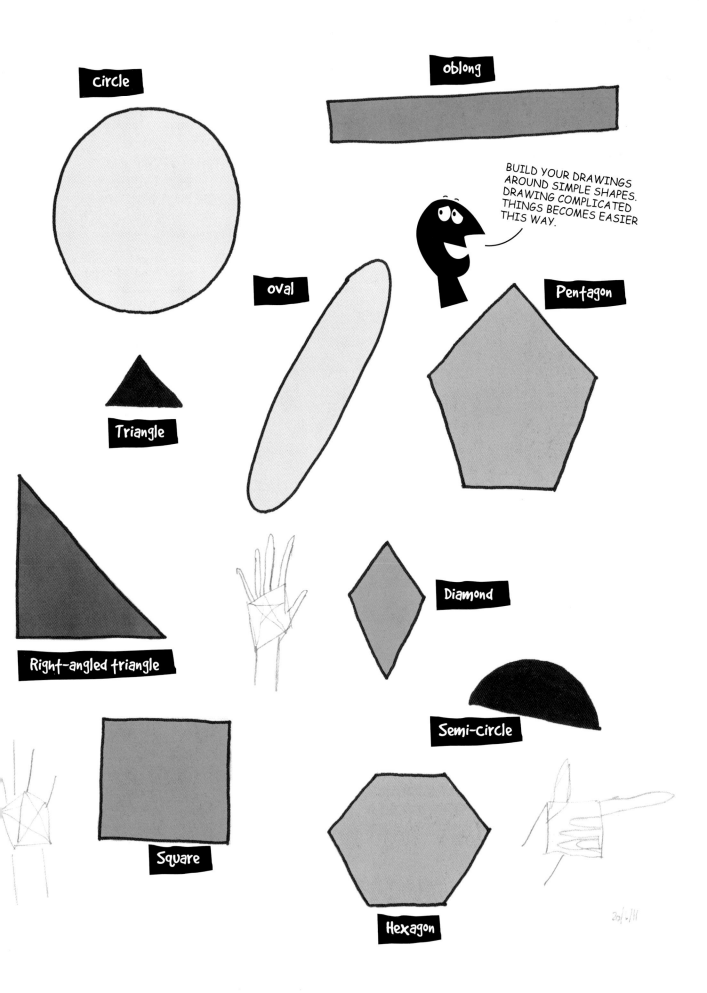

SHAPES ARE EVERYWHERE!
SHAPES CAN BE REPEATED TO MAKE PATTERNS.

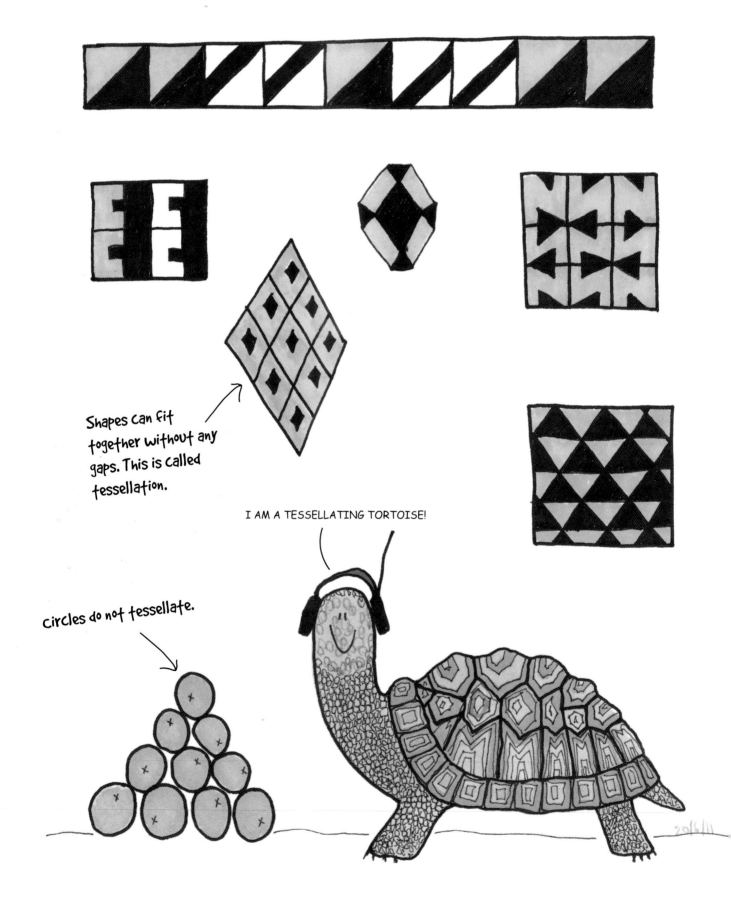

Shapes can fit together without any gaps. This is called tessellation.

I AM A TESSELLATING TORTOISE!

Circles do not tessellate.

Which shapes tessellate?
Create your own shape design.

FISHY SHAPES

ONE SHAPE MAKES A FISH!

1. Draw a diamond.

2. Add a tail.

3. Fins

4. Face

5. Patterns

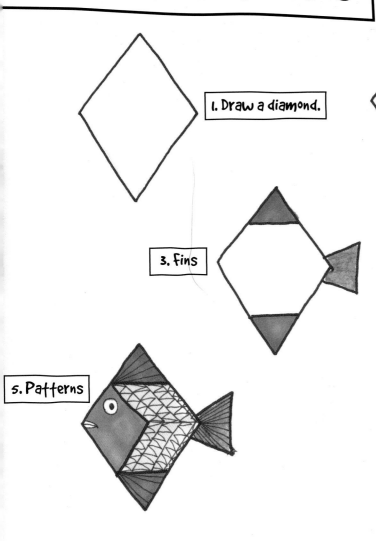

Imagine you are a deep-sea diver.
Draw the shape fish you see on your fantasy
underwater adventure.

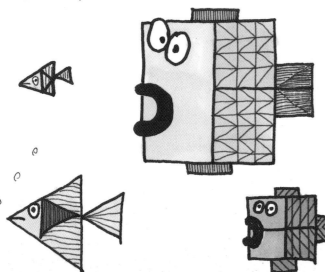

JOINING SHAPES

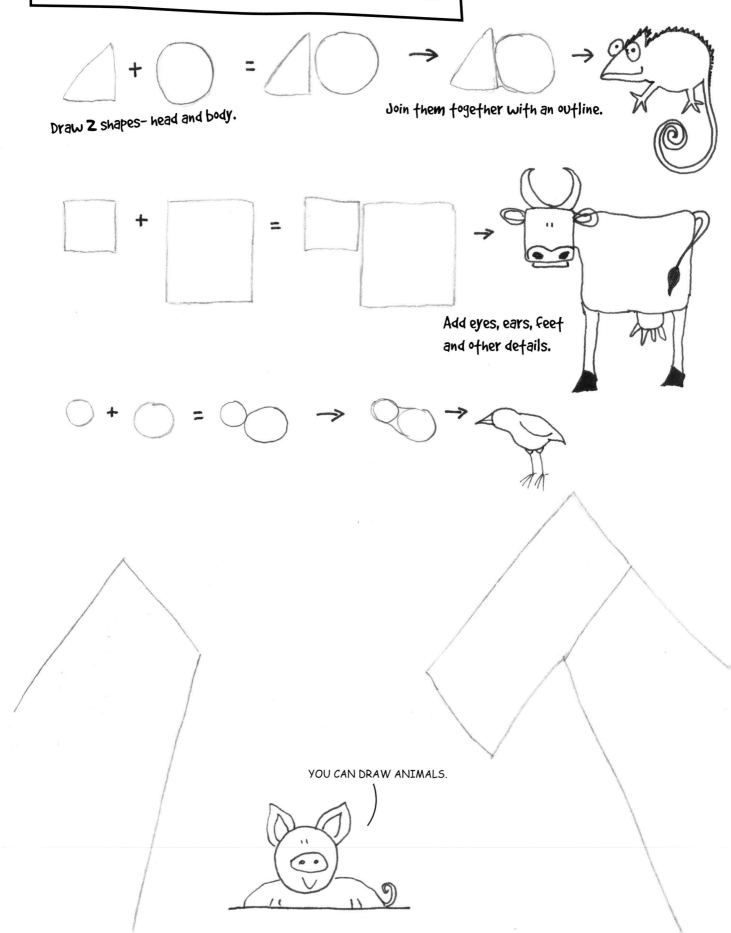

Draw **2** shapes- head and body.

Join them together with an outline.

Add eyes, ears, feet and other details.

YOU CAN DRAW ANIMALS.

Use light guidelines to draw simple shapes.

Join circles to make animal heads and bodies.

ANIMAL PATTERNS

DON'T FORGET TO DRAW PATTERN ON YOUR ANIMALS. THINGS COULD GET CONFUSING!

PATTERNS

WAVY

WHERE CAN YOU SEE THESE PATTERNS?

FLORAL

CHECK

ZIGZAG

PAISLEY

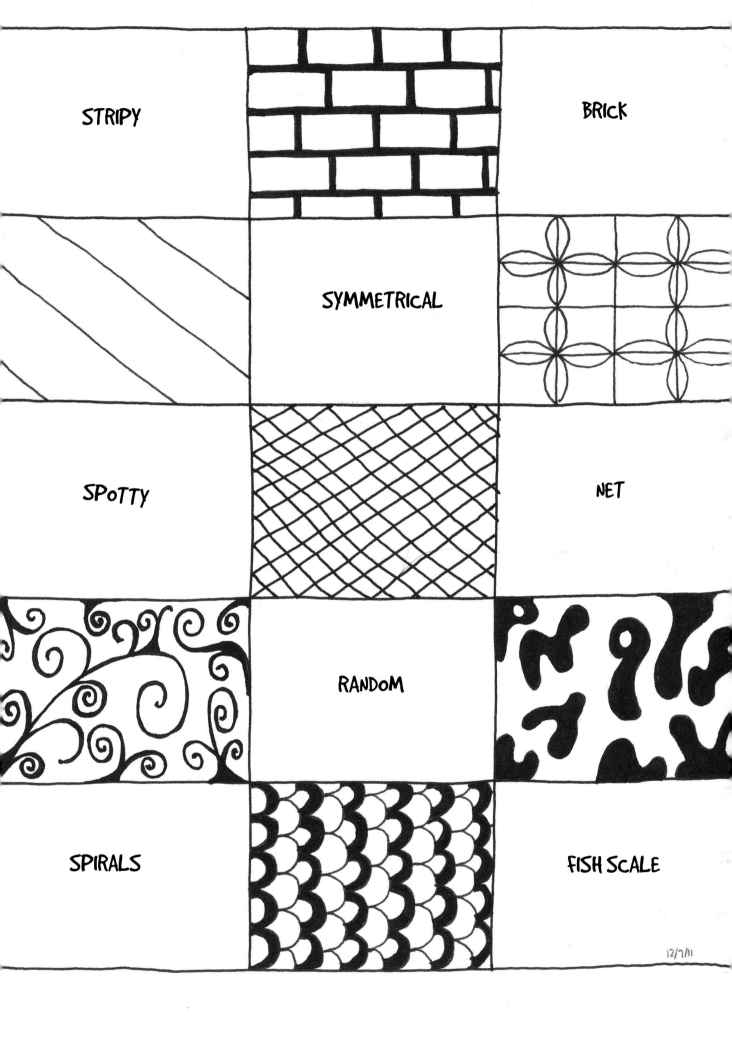

STRIPY

BRICK

SYMMETRICAL

SPOTTY

NET

SPIRALS

RANDOM

FISH SCALE

12/7/11

PATTERNS IN DETAIL

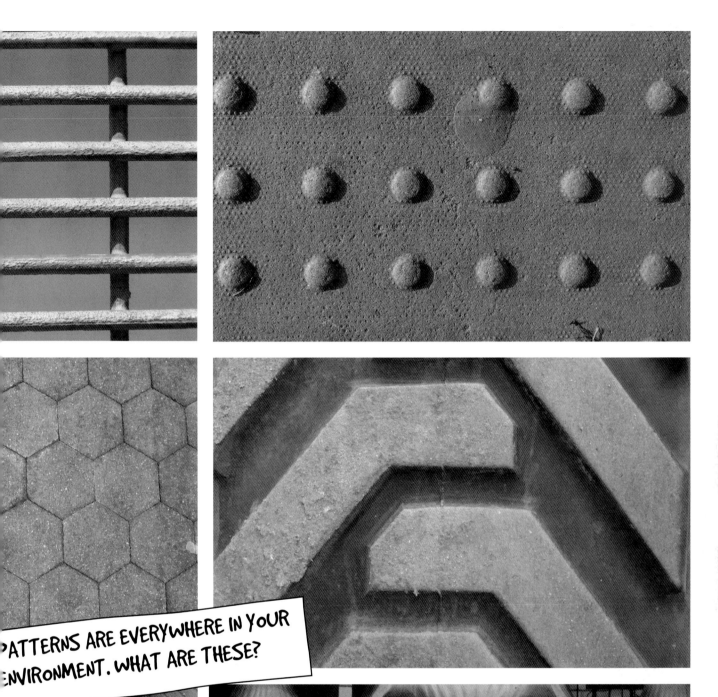

PATTERNS ARE EVERYWHERE IN YOUR ENVIRONMENT. WHAT ARE THESE?

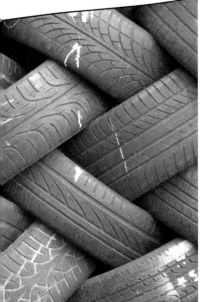

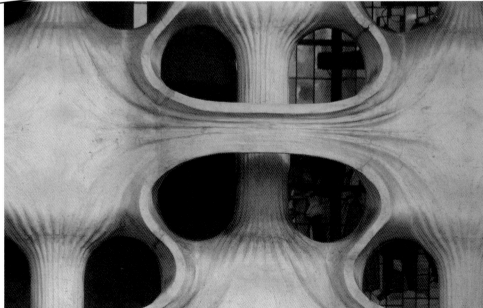

JUMPING PATTERNS

1. DRAW A STRAIGHT LINE.

2. NOW jUMP FROM ONE END TO THE OTHER.

Put a dot in the middle of a line.
Jump from the end of the line to the dot and jump again.
It looks like a mouth!

Lots of dots, lots of jumps!

Try jumping along a curved line.

EYES

An eyeball sits in an eye socket.

The size of the pupil changes depending on how much light there is.

Big pupil = little light

Small pupil = a lot of light

SURPRISE!

A simple way to draw eyes:

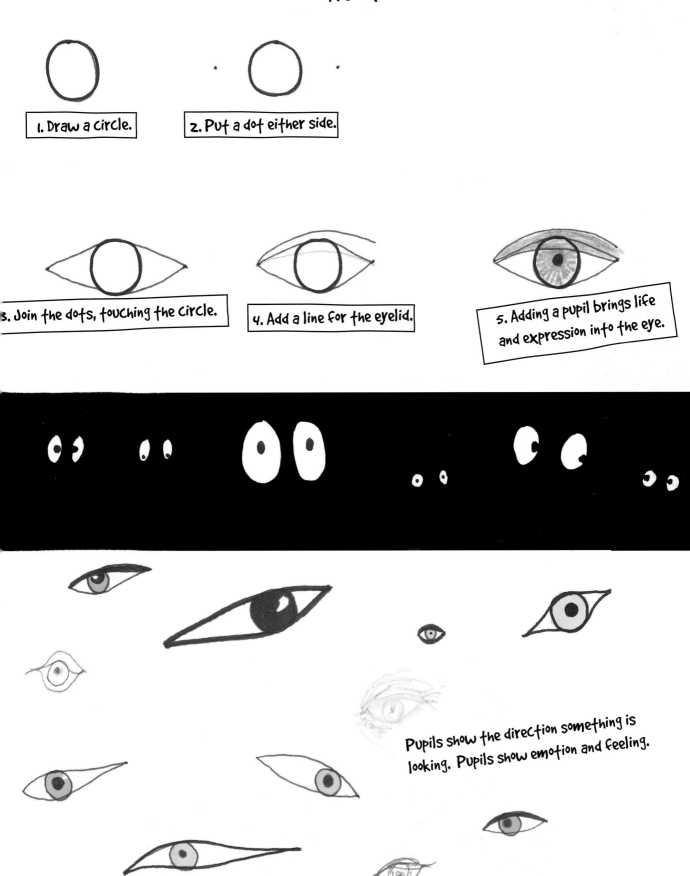

1. Draw a circle.

2. Put a dot either side.

3. Join the dots, touching the circle.

4. Add a line for the eyelid.

5. Adding a pupil brings life and expression into the eye.

Pupils show the direction something is looking. Pupils show emotion and feeling.

Experiment by changing the distance between your dots and circle.

HOW TO DRAW A FACE

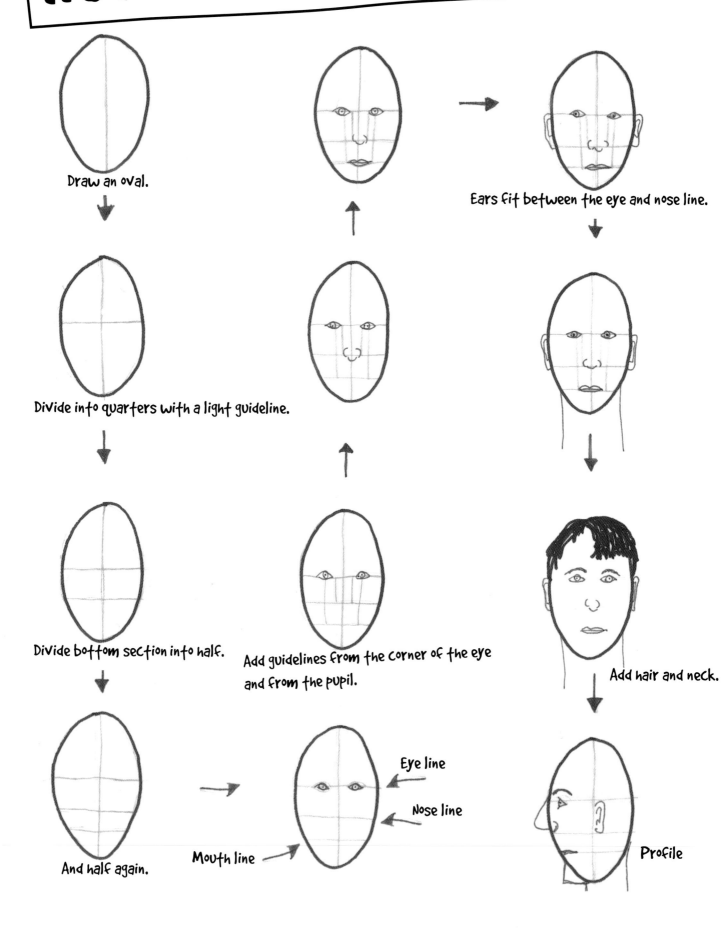

Draw an oval.

Divide into quarters with a light guideline.

Divide bottom section into half.

And half again.

Mouth line

Eye line

Nose line

Add guidelines from the corner of the eye and from the pupil.

Ears fit between the eye and nose line.

Add hair and neck.

Profile

Remember to include tone and detail.
Half close your eyes and the light lines disappear.

IF YOU KNOW THE BASIC RULES OF HOW TO DRAW A FACE YOU CAN PLAY AROUND AND MAKE ALL SORTS OF FACES. CARTOON FACES DO NOT STICK TO THESE RULES.... LOOK AT ME!!

Hair can cover the ears but they are still there!

DRAW A FACE WITHOUT LOOKING

CLOSE YOUR EYES AND DRAW A FACE.
IT LOOKS FUNNY!

8/5/11

Draw a face using one line.

Use one long line.
Take your pen off the paper when you finish your drawing.

WHAT ELSE CAN YOU DRAW IN THIS WAY?

8/5/11

THE BODY

THE HUMAN BODY IS AMAZING.

Your arms outstretched from fingertip to fingertip measures about the same as your height.

An adult head fits into the height of a person about 8 times.

Your elbow touches your waist. →

Your foot fits into your arm.

Your fingertips reach roughly half way down your thighs.

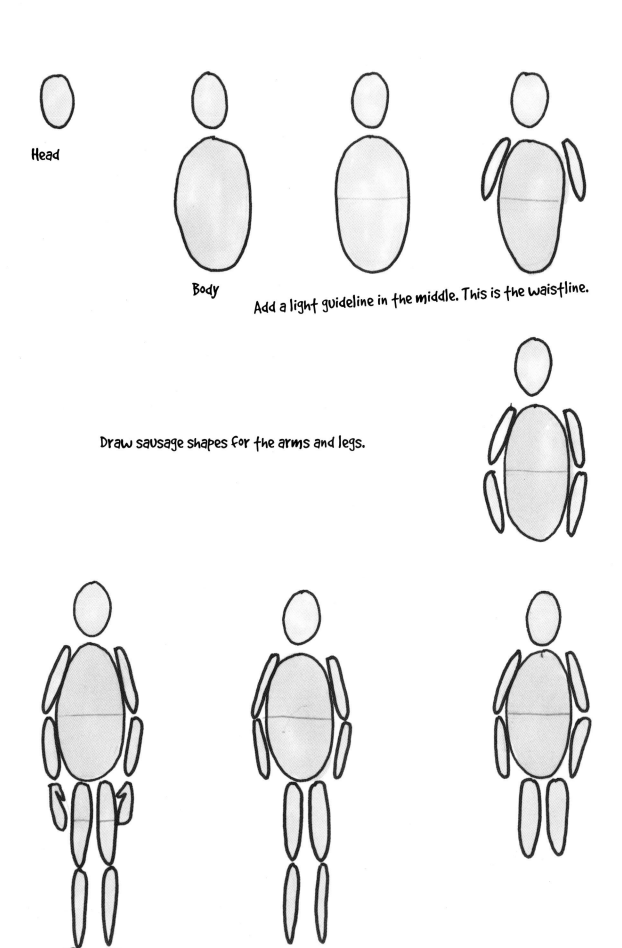

Head

Body

Add a light guideline in the middle. This is the waistline.

Draw sausage shapes for the arms and legs.

GET INTO ACTION

PLAY AROUND WITH SHAPES TO CREATE DIFFERENT ACTIONS, POSITIONS AND MOVEMENT.

Add details and you can create whatever character you like.

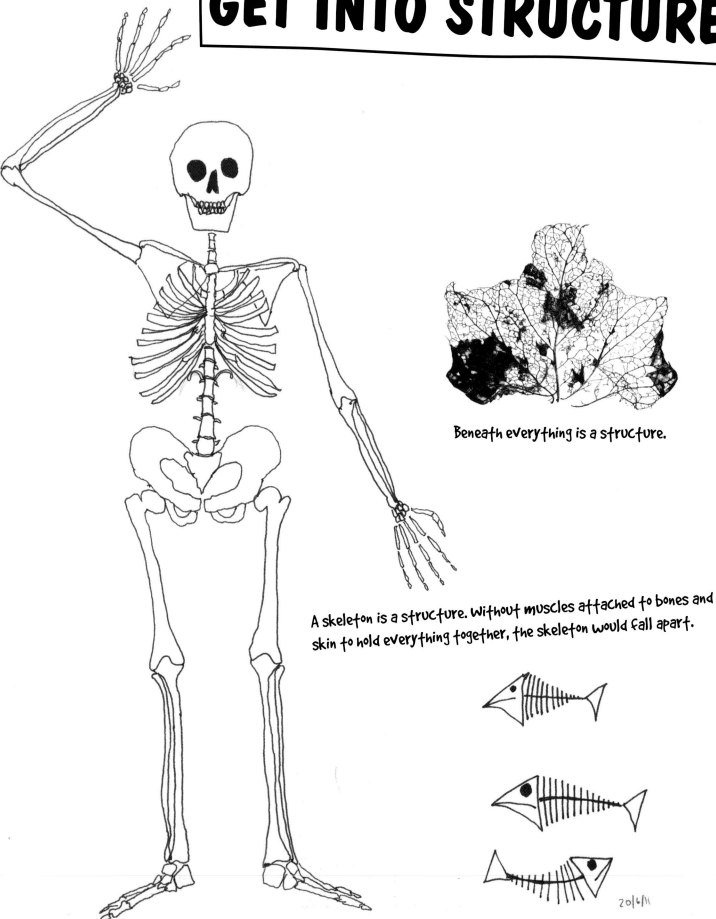

Beneath everything is a structure.

A skeleton is a structure. Without muscles attached to bones and skin to hold everything together, the skeleton would fall apart.

20/6/11

Study bone structure of people and animals to help your drawing.

TEXTURE

TEXTURE DESCRIBES HOW
SOMETHING FEELS.
HOW WOULD YOU DESCRIBE
THESE TEXTURES?
CAN YOU DRAW THEM?

Draw a simple face. No hair.
Add different textures to change the appearance of each person.

CHANGING A SHAPE
FROM 2D INTO 3D

Draw a square.

Draw a dot away from the square
This is called the vanishing point.

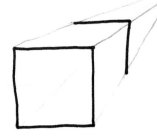

Using guidelines join the corners of
the square to the vanishing point.

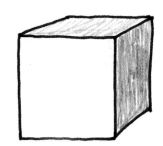

Add dark lines to create your 3D shape.

See through

Cube

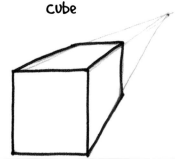

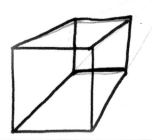

open

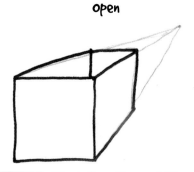

PERSPECTIVE

PERSPECTIVE IS AN ARTISTS' TRICK THAT GIVES DEPTH TO A DRAWING.

Disappearing lines

Vanishing point

Horizon

All lines meet at the vanishing point.

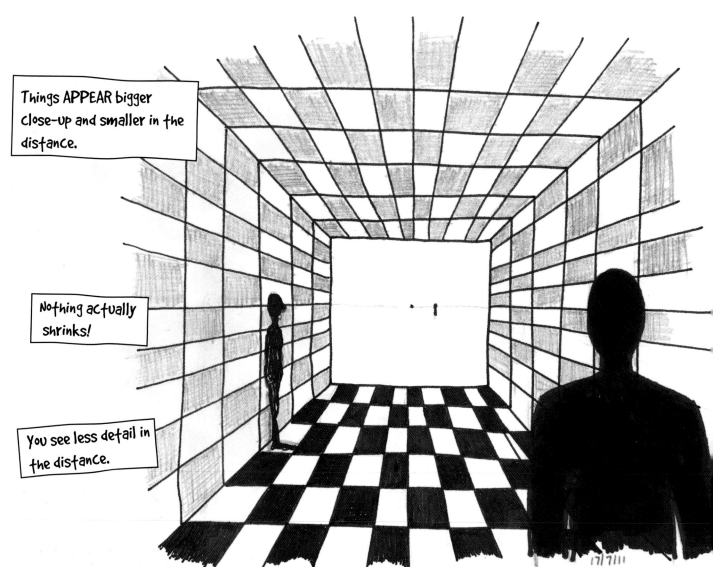

Things APPEAR bigger close-up and smaller in the distance.

Nothing actually shrinks!

You see less detail in the distance.

Where is the vanishing point?

PERSPECTIVE IN LANDSCAPE

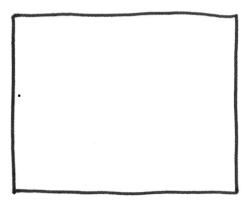

Draw a dot—the vanishing point.

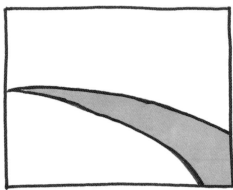

Draw 2 curved lines from the dot, this becomes a path, or road.

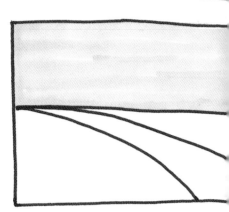

Add the horizon.

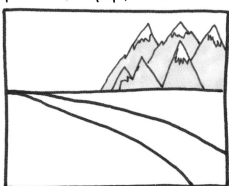

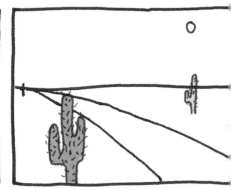

Change direction.

GO ON A JOURNEY INTO YOUR IMAGINATION. DRAW WHAT YOU SEE!

Add a bend.

Lower the horizon = more sky.

Landscape without a road.

Above

Experiment! Draw!

Upside down

close-up

far away

Reflection

Reflection

Magnify

Sideways

Below

DON'T WORRY ABOUT MISTAKES

'Mistake'

Avoid getting upset, scrunching up your work and throwing it away.

Keep calm!!

Making a 'mistake' encourages you to think in a different way.

See it as a positive thing. Be creative and flexible with 'mistakes'.

If you make a mistake blend it into your drawing...

or leave and start again.

Ban erasers (unless you are removing guidelines). If you keep rubbing away your drawing you end up rubbing away your confidence!

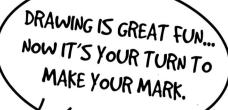

DRAWING IS GREAT FUN... NOW IT'S YOUR TURN TO MAKE YOUR MARK.

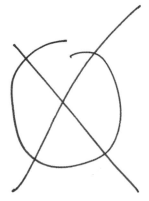

Avoid crossing out. This mark becomes part of your drawing and looks ugly.